51 Reasons I Don't Want Children, 37 Responses I'm Tired of Hearing, & 13 Things About Parenthood That Annoy Me

Jasmine F. Tucker

Copyright © 2021 by Jasmine F. Tucker

All rights reserved. No part of this book may be reproduced or used in any manner without written permission of the copyright owner except for the use of quotations in a book review.

Disclaimer

This book contains my personal thoughts, views, and opinions. It is completely acceptable to disagree with me. I am not trying to pass off my personal opinions as facts. There is nothing wrong with being or wanting to be a parent.

Dedication

For anyone who has ever felt alone in their decision to be childfree,
For anyone who has ever doubted themselves or their decision to be childfree,
For anyone who has not been supported in their decision to be childfree,
For anyone who's angry and tired of explaining themselves,
For anyone who has had to fight to have their voice heard,
I wrote this for us.

Introduction

My name is Jasmine Tucker, I'm from southwest Ohio, and I had a relatively normal childhood. My little brother and I were raised by loving parents in a good school district. Our father had the traditional role of being the sole financial provider, while my mother was the stay-at-home parent. I had several healthy interests and extracurricular activities that my parents encouraged and supported. I had friends to hang out with and a yard to play in. Our family had the occasional struggle here and there, but I was never without a roof over my head or food on my table. We were, and continue to be, a happy family unit. I was well-loved and accepted by everyone in my life. The only thing that was not accepted about me, was my decision to be childfree.

I don't remember the exact day, but sometime around fifteen years old, I decided I did not want to have children. Society didn't like that. It was very lonely growing up knowing that I didn't want children. I had no one in my life that was childfree by choice and nobody supported me or believed me. My decision was not taken seriously. I was just a young, stupid teenager that knew nothing about life and would eventually change her mind. Friends, family, coworkers, and strangers constantly told me I would change my mind, that I would eventually have kids whether-or-not I wanted it, or that I was a horrible person for not wanting kids. It was very difficult to be raised in a society that pushes women to have children. My culture conditions us from a young age to believe that having babies is our purpose in life and that we would be worthless without the desire to reproduce. I have spent the last fifteen years defending my decision to everyone who has ever asked me if I had or wanted kids. It has been exhausting and maddening.

This year (2021), I turned thirty years old and I've noticed that I'm not getting as much backlash about this topic as I used to, which I am grateful for. I'm sure I'll still get badgered about my choice for the rest of my life, but it seems like the fifteen years in between age fifteen and age thirty were the worst. But even though the people surrounding me seem to have finally accepted my decision and have begun to believe me, I'm still angry. I'm mad that I had to fight so hard to be believed. I'm mad that it took so long for people to take me seriously. I'm mad at society for treating me this way. I'm mad at my friends and family for dismissing me so easily. I'm mad that I was told that I was a waste of a human being, that I had less value because I didn't want to use my uterus. Nobody should have to be treated this way.

So, I could say I wrote this book because I was tired of repeating myself and wanted something to hand people who asked questions. I could say that I wrote this book because I saw a lack of childfree books available and I wanted to add another one to the list. I could say I wanted to share my experiences, share what it was like to grow up childfree. I could say that I wanted to help normalize the decision to not have kids. But mostly, I wrote this book because I am angry, and I wanted the world to know. I wrote this book because I am saddened and frustrated by how society treated me, and I want society to know. I wrote this because I felt alone and I want others who have gone through similar experiences to know that they aren't alone.

For easy reading, this book is split into four sections. The first section, *Reasons I Don't Want*

Children, is where I list and elaborate on a few of the endless reasons I do not want to have kids or be a mother. The second section, *Responses I'm Tired Of Hearing*, contains some of the more common responses I have received thus far in my life. The third section, *Things About Parenthood That Annoy Me*, is a collection of things that annoy me personally, but I feel that other childfree individuals would relate to, as well. The fourth section, *Honorable Mentions*, has topics that do not quite fall into the categories of reasons, responses, or annoying things, but I still feel they are worthy of inclusion.

Reasons I Don't Want Children

Reason #1
I Don't Want Them

Society tends to forget that this is the only reason I need for choosing a childfree life. I don't owe anyone any further explanation. If this were my only reason for not wanting children, it would still be a good enough reason. Not wanting something is a valid reason not to get something.

Reason #2
Commitment

This is probably my biggest reason for not wanting to have children. They are a huge time commitment, at least eighteen years. Even then, your responsibilities as a parent don't seem to end the day your child becomes a legal adult. Personally, I wasn't able to move out of my parents' house until I was twenty-three years old. Meaning, my parents financially supported me for twenty-three years instead of only eighteen. Once you become a parent, you are a parent for the rest of your life.

But even at the minimum, eighteen years is an incredibly long time. Assuming I have one hundred years to live, I have already spent thirty of them. And as an adult, I spend most of my days working. Even my days off are filled with obligations such as grocery shopping or mowing the lawn. Most people, myself included, get very little time to do activities that they actually enjoy. When I do get free time in my daily life, I prefer to fill it with things I love. I don't want to waste my free time or spend eighteen years of my incredibly brief life span raising a child.

I may not be an adolescent anymore, but I am

still young and someday I will be too old to enjoy certain things. I refuse to waste the years I'm young enough to travel, and be wild, by doing boring things like changing diapers.

Reason #3
Expensive

The cost of raising a child can vary drastically depending on many factors. But no matter how wealthy you are, how old you are, or what the current economy is like, we can all agree that raising a child can be extremely expensive. At the time of this writing, the current economy makes it very difficult for someone in my wealth class to afford the expenses related to raising children. Which is one of the many reasons I have chosen not to have kids.

My generation was raised hearing things like *"Don't buy things you can't afford!"* and now the older generations seem to be surprised when birth rates decline because people are choosing not to have children they can't afford. My husband and I may live fairly comfortably, but the majority of our paychecks go toward living expenses. The only reason we are able to build savings or take time off for vacations is because we do not have any children. The cost of even one child is something we could not handle. Even if I wanted children, I have never in my life been in a situation where I could financially support even one dependent. I would much rather spend any extra cash on myself or my pets, anyway.

Reason #4
Tokophobia

Tokophobia, the fear of pregnancy, is one of my greatest fears. Both the act of carrying a baby inside me and the resulting eighteen years of responsibility afterwards. Being so terrified of pregnancy has caused me to go to extreme lengths to prevent it, and I take mine and my partners forms of contraceptives very seriously. The amount of side effects and risks associated with pregnancy horrifies me and I don't think enough people take it into consideration when deciding whether-or-not to become pregnant. Of course, some people have incredibly easy pregnancies and births but that is not the case for everyone.

Pregnancy can have a huge array of side effects such as, but not limited to: morning sickness, fatigue, increased urination, mood swings, constipation, cramping, nasal congestion, varicose veins, backaches, sleep loss, gingivitis, yeast infection, incontinence, vaginal discharge, food sensitivities, gas, heartburn, itchy skin, restless leg syndrome, excessive hair growth, acne, and sore breasts. Nine months of symptoms like these can cause complete exhaustion in most expectant mothers and by the end, many women await their due date eagerly. Nine months is an incredibly long time and I know I certainly could not handle it. Gestation for humans is dangerous and can even become a life-threatening condition. It is a small percentage of people who die as a result of pregnancy, but I still don't think it is worth risking my life just to have a baby.

The list of things that can go wrong during childbirth is just as massive as the pregnancy side effects list. Childbirth is also a dangerous activity that can cause the death of either the mother, the baby, or both. I would never risk the possibility of having my spouse become a single parent in the event of my death during childbirth. Besides the fear of death, another of my fears related to childbirth is the possibility of tearing during labor. The vagina, perineum and even the anus can tear during this process. In extremely rare cases, the clitoris can tear as well. I like my clitoris, vagina, perineum, and anus just the way they are and I have no desire to risk their health and safety just to have a baby. The cervix itself has to dilate to ten centimeters and I don't think most people understand how large that is. The head of an infant is massive, and my vagina trembles in fear at the idea of pushing one out.

Pregnancy ends after nine months but some side effects stick around for a much longer. Not only is there eighteen years of responsibility to look forward to, long-term side effects of pregnancy can include sagging breasts, weight gain, increased shoe size, stretch marks, incontinence, and tooth loss. Having a baby is not for the faint of heart, and I am someone who is not cut out for it.

Reason #5
Overpopulation

At the time of this writing (2021), the current estimated human population is 7.9 billion. That number continues to rise every year. Some say the human-race is overpopulated and others say that the planet could handle billions more and that the real problem is unequal distribution of resources. Either way, nearly 8 billion humans are more than enough, in my opinion. The Earth and all its inhabitants (humans included) are suffering because of our massive population, and I would rather not add to our numbers.

Reason #6
I Believe Choosing To Have Biological Children Is Selfish

I have yet to be presented with a reason to have a biological child that is not for the benefit of the parents or someone else who is already alive. I cannot justify creating a sentient being for the sake of my personal benefit.

"I want to be a mom."

"I want someone to take care of me when I'm old"

"I want bigger tax returns"

"I want someone to pass my family name or business too"

"I want to make more (insert religion).*"*

"I want to make more (insert race).*"*

"I want my life to have meaning."

"I want to fix my relationship or make my spouse happy."

"I want to make my parents happy."

These are all excuses that benefit someone other than the child being born. I can't think of any reason to bring a human being into existence that isn't for selfish reasons. Kids don't have any say on whether-or-not they are born into this world full of pain and suffering. Maybe if we lived in a perfect utopia where a life of joy and happiness is a guarantee for every child, this would be a different discussion.

Reason #7
Undesirable Society

The society that I currently live in is highly capitalistic, patriarchal, racist, ableist, and heteronormative. This is a society that I do not enjoy existing in and certainly not a society I would ever want to raise a child in. While we have made great strides in recent years to better ourselves as a civilization, I believe we are far from being perfect. It will be an incredibly long time before humanity can come together to form a society that has each other's best interests at heart. And it certainly won't happen in my lifetime.

Reason #8
Diapers

I have never changed a diaper in my life, and I never will. Human feces are disgusting and I do everything I can to avoid it. Baby poop, in particular, has an insanely powerful stench. Handling strong, unpleasant smells is not something I deal with very well. If a smell is too intense, it can make my stomach queasy, and I have to leave the area before I vomit.

Diapers are also fairly expensive and disposable ones, like any disposable product, are bad for the environment. Disposable diapers can take hundreds of years to decompose in a landfill. Reusable diapers are much better for the planet but can still be expensive upfront even though they are cheaper in the long run.

If you need another reason to hate diapers, take a moment to do an internet search for images of "diaper blowouts." Basically, diapers are gross and expensive and I don't want to deal with them at all.

Reason #9
Kids Are Sticky

Have you ever grabbed a public door handle, and it turned out to be sticky? Super gross, right? That's what it's like handling young children. Is it sucker residue? Gummy bears? Boogers? Urine? Feces? You'll never know.

Reason #10
Kids Are Boring

Kids and everything related to kids such as TV shows, movies, books, parties, school, and homework, are so boring. I enjoy adult entertainment and activities, and there is just no way I would ever want to trade that for child-friendly activities.

Reason #11
Why Bring A Kid Into Such A Violent World?

There is no doubt that our world is full of good and compassionate people. Our world is beautiful and filled with indescribable wonders. It is truly a magical place. But the fact is, it is also full of cruelty and violence. There are people who are greedy and barbaric, who only care about themselves. The planet itself is full of dangerous creatures and natural disasters. Mother Nature is a truly savage mistress. And while I enjoy being alive, my life is at risk every single moment I draw breath. I live in a country where gun violence and physical assaults happen daily.

Every day I live could be the day I get kidnapped, trafficked, raped, or murdered. Every breath I take could introduce me to a deadly virus or bacteria. I risk death every time I drive my vehicle. The very sky itself could reach down in the form of a tornado and end it all in an instant. Why would I ever choose to bring a child into such a violent world?

Reason #12
I Would Be A Bad Mother

Me not wanting to be a mother would make me a bad mother. Nobody deserves to be raised by somebody who doesn't want to be a parent. Every child deserves to grow up feeling wanted, and I could not provide that.

Reason #13
Vomit

Vomit is incredibly disgusting and simply seeing or smelling it can cause me to throw up the contents of my stomach as well. This is called "sympathetic vomiting" and it occurs when the sight, sound or smell of another person vomiting causes you to become nauseated and vomit. If I am in the same room as someone else who is puking, I have to leave as quickly as possible, before the smell can make me queasy. Seeing as babies and young children throw up quite often, being a sympathetic vomiter would be very inconvenient for a mother. Even if I didn't have the urge to hurl every time someone else did, vomit is gross and I don't want to deal with it any more than absolutely necessary. Best to just not birth a barf machine at all.

Reason #14
Kids Are Bad For The Environment

Having a child means producing yet another human that will put a strain on this planet's already dwindling natural resources. The majority of us live in societies that make it nearly impossible to exist without harming the environment. My own existence is terrible for the environment even though I try my best to reduce the damage I do to the Earth while I'm alive. I hate that even though I eat a plant-based diet, drive an eco-friendly car, recycle, re-purpose, compost, and reduce plastic usage, my life will leave a scar on this planet. I wish I could do more to reverse the damage the last few generations have done to the world, but I can't. I wish I could make large polluters care about the planet over profits, but I can't. All I can do is live my life as eco-friendly as possible while encouraging others to do the same. Kids are bad for the environment and I care about the planet enough to not bring more polluters onto it.

Reason #15
Spontaneity

I love being able to roll out of bed on my days off and plan a spur of the moment day trip. I love planning a last minute overnight camping trip or waiting until the day of to make plans. Being able to be spontaneous is exciting, why would I want to give that up? Having to hire and pay for a babysitter would make being spontaneous a lot more difficult. I love being impulsive and don't want to give that up just to have a baby.

Reason #16
I Like Having Nice Things

I'm no millionaire, but I enjoy having nice things. Breakable things. I enjoy collecting and displaying crystals and minerals. Which can be quite an expensive hobby and many specimens can be rather fragile. Having a child would require me to either not display my collection at all or to childproof how I display them, and I would prefer not to do either of those options.

My house also contains expensive and breakable non-collectible items such as iPhones, television, laptop, vehicles, furniture, books, game consoles, and appliances. I don't want a child who doesn't understand the concept of money to destroy these items. I also own dangerous items like guns, knives, Tazers, and swords. Some of these are for self defense and others are for decoration. Besides being able to cause a child harm, I don't want them broken either.

To prevent a child from harming themselves or my possessions, I would have to spend time and money on childproofing my house. Things such as locking cabinet doors, hiding chemicals, anchoring furniture, putting bumpers on sharp edges, covering outlets. The list is never ending. Besides being an inconvenience, I genuinely don't think my half-awake self could unlock a childproofed toilet in the middle of the night. To avoid these hassles and keep my valuables safe, I simply won't have any children.

Reason #17
What If They Are Allergic To My Pets?

I take the term "forever home" very seriously. My pets are my family. Once I adopt them into my life, I am responsible for them until the day they die. I absolutely cannot risk having to re-home my family members if my child is allergic to them.

Reason #18
I Love Taking Vacations

I am privileged enough to afford multiple vacations per year. Both my husband and I take a week off in the spring and a week off in the fall for vacation. We can't always afford to go anywhere exciting, but we still make sure to take this time off from work. Even if it turns into a "stay-cation," having this time away from the stresses of our jobs is wonderful for our mental health. We think it is extremely important to take care of ourselves and our health before our jobs. We refuse to overwork ourselves for a company that would replace us in a day if we died tomorrow. So vacations have turned into a priority for us, no matter our budget.

Traveling is one of my biggest enjoyments in life. Seeing new places and going on adventures make me feel truly alive. Even if I can't make it farther than a state or two away, traveling will always be important to me. Plus, it's nice to get away from the little hick town I grew up and still live in. Having children would put my vacations in danger of either not existing at all or requiring them to be kid-friendly. Even if I could still afford multiple vacations a year with a child, I don't want to spend my vacations doing kid-friendly activities. Events that are appropriate for children are often full of other people's disgusting kids or are extremely boring. I have too many things on my travel bucket list to waste any time on activities I do not enjoy.

Reason #19
Shared Interests

What if my child and I have no shared interests and I have to pretend to like the things they like for eighteen years? Can't risk it.

Reason #20
I Am An Introvert

I always have been and always will be an introvert. I truly enjoy spending my time being alone and doing things by myself. Making sure to have at least one day a week to myself, to recharge and prepare for the next week of socialization. Having a child would drastically reduce the amount of alone time I would get. And even though extroverts are wonderful people that I love being around, I don't think I could handle raising an extroverted child.

Reason #21
Quality Time With Spouse

My husband and I spend a considerable amount of time together. We live in the same house and work at the same job. At our job, we work the same shift at the same location. Our daily routine involves waking up at the same time, eating breakfast together, carpooling to work, spending the majority of our eight-hour shift together, carpooling home, making and eating dinner, and going to bed about the same time each night. We run errands on the weekends and take vacations together. So even though we spend a little more time with each other than typical couples, I still enjoy being around him. Having a child would take away from the time I get to spend with my spouse and I don't want that to happen.

Reason #22
Losing My Identity To Motherhood

I've seen this happen to friends, and am afraid it would happen to me as well. Sometimes being a parent becomes your entire existence and you forget who you were before having children. I don't want to become someone who loses their identity to motherhood. I struggle with my identity enough as it is, even at my age. Some people can get so wrapped up in being a parent, they forget how to be anything else. It's a struggle many parents have to face, and it's something I wouldn't handle very well.

Reason #23
Too Many Children Need Adopting

There are millions of orphans and foster children across the globe waiting to be adopted. In my opinion, each one of them is a reason not to bring another human into the world. There are so many children that are desperate for a loving family. I understand it's cheaper to make your own baby than to adopt one, but I think it is incredibly selfish to get pregnant deliberately, knowing there are so many kids who already exist that need homes. The term "adopt, don't shop" should apply to humans, as well as animals. Please choose adoption over reproduction.

Reason #24
Mom Shaming

I don't want to be a mom because I don't want to deal with the other parents and the associated "mom-shaming." It doesn't matter what you do, or the choices you make regarding raising your child, there will always be other moms who shame you for your decisions. Moms who will tell you that you are a bad parent for choosing formula over breastfeeding, even though both options result in a well-fed baby. Moms who will shame you for choosing non-organic food over organic, even though not everyone can afford organic.

Whether you choose to be a stay-at-home parent or pay for daycare, other moms will shame both options. There are a million more examples. Many people seem to forget that every parent and every child is an individual and there is not a single perfect way to raise a kid. Parents should strive to do their best to provide for their children and love them unconditionally. Nobody is perfect, and it is okay to make mistakes.

Reason #25
Kids Put Strain On Relationships

No matter how strong your relationship is, having children is stressful and can put a strain on any couple. I am very confident in how strong and healthy my marriage is, but no relationship is perfect. There will always be bumps along the road, but why would I want to add the stress of having children to my road?

Reason #26
Custody

I don't want to deal with custody battles in the event of a divorce.

Reason #27
The Possibility Of Child Loss

Because I do not have children, I have no idea and will never have any idea what it is like to experience the loss of a child. It is a pain that I will never be able to comprehend. But I have had to live through my fair share of the deaths of loved ones, both human and animal. Losing family members is incredibly painful and when you view your pets as family, their deaths can be just as heartbreaking.

But more than once I have had to deal with the unexpected, premature deaths of personal pets that I had raised and viewed as my children. Their passings were and still are, incredibly painful experiences for me. If dealing with the loss of a pet that I view as a child is so difficult to handle, I cannot imagine what it is like to live through the death of a human child. I do not want to have children because I am terrified of the pain of child loss. It is a suffering that I honestly believe would destroy me.

Reason #28
I Don't Want To Give Up My Spare Bedroom

Currently, my husband and I live in a three-bedroom house. One bedroom for our bed and clothing, one bedroom for my stuff and one bedroom for his stuff. So we each have a space for ourselves and the things we like. I use my room for writing, yoga, and displaying my collectibles. It is also good for our relationship to be able to spend time apart doing separate hobbies.

Adding even one child to our lives would mean that we would no longer have our personal rooms anymore, and that is something I do not want to give up. Having a space dedicated to just me without a bed or dresser taking up most of the room has been wonderful for my mental health. And it is something I am not willing to give up.

Reason #29
Chores

I already hate doing chores. My job requires cleaning, and I don't want to come home to do more chores. I have to force myself to do any household tasks because they are incredibly boring and repetitive. Chores are a truly never-ending task, and adding even one child to the house would drastically increase the number of general chores that I would have to do. More clothes to wash, more dishes to scrub, more picking up and putting things away. I don't want children because I despise chores and I don't want to do any more than I absolutely have to. If I could afford a maid, I would certainly have one.

Reason #30
I Cannot Handle A Special Needs Child

Giving birth to a baby or adopting a child means you are risking the possibility of having a child with special needs. Even adopting an older child doesn't guarantee that they will be "typical." This is something that I don't think I have the ability to handle. Every special needs child deserves to be loved and raised by someone who can give them everything they need to live their best life. I am not one of those people.

Having people in my life with special needs children has allowed me to see just how difficult it can be sometimes. These parents end up doing so much extra for their children, going above and beyond on a daily basis. They, of course, would do anything for their kids and care for them out of love. But sometimes that care can be twice as time-consuming and expensive as a "typical" child. Some of these children can never be truly independent and will rely on their parents for care indefinitely. These parents are true saints for what they do, but I can clearly see the toll it takes on them. I don't have the strength required to be a special needs parent.

Reason #31
Drool

Babies are known for their excessive drooling. I won't even adopt any dog breeds that produce large amounts of saliva. I'm certainly not going to want to deal with baby drool.

Reason #32
New Baby Smell

For some reason, a tremendous amount of people seem to think that the "new baby smell" infants have, is a wonderful perk of being around babies. I think babies smell horrendous even when they are clean, and it's not something I would want to live with.

Reason #33
Babies Are Fragile

The most important and expensive item I use in my day-to-day life is my smartphone. For me and most people in this society, it is very important and has my whole life on it. This is an incredibly valuable item and I have to use a practically indestructible, shock-proof, water-proof, dust-proof, everything-proof case on it because I drop it so many times each day. You can't put a protective case on a baby. If I were to be put in charge of keeping an infant alive, I don't think I could. I would probably drop it, like I drop my phone.

Reason #34
Doctors Visits

I despise taking myself to the doctor, and only go if it is an absolute necessity. Having a child would drastically increase the amount of time I spend in doctor's offices. Pregnancy requires many appointments, newborns need regular visits, and even older kids seem to get sick fairly often as well. Maybe I would have a healthy child that rarely needs to see a doctor, or maybe I'd have a kid with health problems that need constant visits. It's just a risk I'm not willing to take.

Reason #35
I'm A Slow Runner

Kids run off all the time. I frequently see parents chasing after their children. Sometimes it can be a life or death situation, having to catch up to them before they run into the road or off a cliff. We live in a dangerous world. Running has never been a talent of mine and I honestly don't think I could catch a kid who needs to be caught. Even in my best physical shape, I could hardly outrun a turtle. And I don't think I could be a parent who uses a leash on a child. Besides being embarrassing for everyone involved, they can't be used 24/7. I don't want to have kids because I'm afraid I'm too slow to keep them from running into traffic.

Reason #36
I Hate Cooking

Sometimes I'd rather starve than to have to make myself another meal. Cooking is such a ridiculously repetitive task. Every day, multiple times a day, until I die. And then you have to do the dishes afterward as well. I love eating at restaurants because somebody else does the cooking and cleaning. If I could afford it, I would hire a personal chef to cook every single one of my meals. Having a child would mean that not only would I have to do more cooking, I would also have to do healthy cooking. A balanced diet with vegetables and such. Outrageous. Not to mention, kids are weirdly picky about their food. They are also incredibly wasteful and messy eaters. I don't want to cook for children, eat their leftovers, or clean spilled food off of everything.

Reason #37
I Don't Have Enough Patience

I used to have the patience of a saint. Then I grew up and spent years in the retail and hospitality industries. Working with the public for an extended period of time has left me with hardly any patience. And somehow my tolerance levels seem to continue dwindling with each passing year. Children require vast amounts of patience and I just simply do not have enough.

Reason #38
Kids Are Creepy

If a kid came into my bedroom in the middle of the night and asked me for a glass of water, I would probably scream and punch it in its face. I'm not ashamed to admit that I am a grown woman who is afraid of the dark. My cats already terrify me enough with the ungodly noises they make at night. Adding a child to the mix is not something I can handle.

Reason #39
Auditory Sensory Overload

I occasionally get overwhelmed by situations that are too loud or have repetitive, annoying noises. Children are known for being loud, annoying, and repetitive. Babies cry and kids scream, it's normal but I absolutely cannot handle it. Newborn cries, in particular, are one of the worst sounds on the planet and I will never understand how mothers are able to deal with it. Sometimes just being in an overly crowded public area with too many sources of sound can raise my heart rate, force me to plug my ears, and take a few deep breaths. Having more than one source of conversation, (for example, talking on the phone while a movie is playing in the same room) will cause me to be unable to focus on anything at all. I don't think I can handle the extreme auditory sensory overload that comes with having children.

Reason #40
Personal Chauffeur

I hate driving. My spouse hates driving. One of our weekly arguments is about who's turn it is to drive to the grocery store. Kids can't drive for sixteen years or more, which means over a decade of being someone else's personal chauffeur. Doctor visits, after-school activities, sports, dates, shopping, or any number of other activities. Wasting even more of my time driving someone else around sounds awful. As well as the motherly concern for newly licensed teens. I'd be spending half my time wondering if my child is being safe or if they are driving as recklessly as I did at that age.

Reason #41
Climate Crisis

Whether you believe in or deny it, our planet is facing a climate crisis that has already begun to affect us. Future generations face having to survive on a planet damaged by countless individuals that did not care about the consequences of their actions. I refuse to bring a child into existence to live on a planet with such an uncertain environmental future.

Reason #42
Sleep

I thoroughly enjoy sleeping in and sleeping uninterrupted. Kids are known to ruin that. Kids can have you up at all hours of the night or day. Newborns need near-constant care. Young children have bad dreams or need glasses of water. Teens can sneak in or out during the night. I don't want to deal with any of that; I get bothered enough in the middle of the night by my pets or my bladder. I enjoy going to bed whenever I want and sleeping in until noon. I will not ruin that by having a baby.

Reason #43
Sex

It's no secret that having children changes your sex life, and not always for the better. Being able to afford housing away from my parents or roommates has been excellent for my sex life. Sharing a house with only my spouse allows the freedom to participate in sexual activities anywhere and anytime at any volume on my property. Not having to wait until we have the house to ourselves is fantastic, since we have the house to ourselves practically all the time. I don't want to have to go back to containing my sexual activities to a bedroom or to certain times of the day just because I share a house with a child.

Reason #44
Personal Space

I already have an issue with personal space, and kids just absolutely do not understand or respect other people's personal space. Unnecessary physical contact is not something I'm a fan of. I'm not a hugger, handshakes are gross and leg touching on busses is one of my worst fears. Children do not care about anybody's personal space. They will crawl all over you and shove their dirty little faces in yours. And they will do absolutely anything to join you in the bathroom. Sitting on a toilet, trying to pee in peace, and having a toddler scream bloody murder because they wanted to join me, was one moment that cemented my decision to be childfree. I cannot have children because I need my personal spacc.

Reason #45
Clutter

I appreciate having a nice, tidy house. Just having two adults and five pets living in my home creates enough clutter to drive me crazy. I don't want to deal with the added clutter a child would bring.

Reason #46
Family History Of Dangerous Pregnancies

Besides the fact that normal pregnancies can be difficult, I have a family history of dangerous pregnancies. My mother told my sibling and me our birth stories many times over our childhoods, and honestly, they terrified me. My brother and I are our mother's only children, and both of our births were traumatic and dangerous. Severe complications from each labor resulted in her doctor recommending sterilization for fear that future pregnancies might be life-threatening. My grandmother had several pregnancies, most of which did not come to term. She suffered through multiple miscarriages and one medically necessary abortion. My great-grandmother had unspecified difficulties reproducing as well.

I have never experienced pregnancy, but why would I want to knowing that I have a family history of difficult and dangerous pregnancies? With a personal history of extremely difficult menstrual cycles, I'm fairly certain any pregnancy I might experience would be nowhere close to textbook. I have also previously broken my tailbone, which can increase the likelihood of re-breaking it during labor. Knowing my personal and family history about menstruation and pregnancy, I would never risk getting pregnant for fear of experiencing similar severe conditions or even death.

Reason #47

Religion

Though raised religious, I have begun to doubt the religion I grew up in and the uncertainty only increases as time goes on. How am I supposed to know what religion to raise a child in if I am unsure of my own beliefs? I do not think I am qualified to answer the questions every child inevitably has about religion, and there is something to be said about not teaching children religion at all. Perhaps we should wait until they are adults and allow them to choose the religion they prefer.

Reason #48
Raising A Child With Social Media I Didn't Have

I was born in 1991 and didn't receive my first cell phone until I was a senior in high school. It was a flip phone that didn't have access to the internet and I had to share it with my brother. I also didn't have any kind of social media account until I signed up for Facebook in 2009. So, while I use the internet and social media every day now, I have no idea what it's like to grow up with it. Social media has a lot of value and is entertaining, but there are quite a few downsides to it as well and I wouldn't have the first clue how to guide a child through that. Even as an adult, it is incredibly easy to be bullied online and I'm sure it can be even worse for kids. I'm glad I am not faced with the responsibility of teaching kids how to navigate the internet.

Reason #49
School Shootings

As every American knows, this country has a problem with school shootings and gun violence in general. Sending my child to a public school would terrify me for fear they might get injured or killed. I don't want to have a child just to fear for their lives at a public school since home-schooling wouldn't be an option for me.

Special thanks to all the teachers out there who truly care about their students, the ones who go above and beyond to make a difference. You aren't paid enough.

Reason #50
I Haven't Fulfilled My Own Dreams Yet

Parents make tremendous amounts of sacrifices for their children and end up putting their dreams on hold while raising offspring. Often waiting until retirement to do things they couldn't do while supporting kids. Sometimes, parents never get the chance to achieve the goals they had before reproducing. I am nowhere near fulfilling all the hopes and dreams I have for my own life. I have quite a few long-term goals I may not achieve for many years. Putting my dreams on hold, for any reason, is something I absolutely will not consider. I have worked hard for years to acquire the possessions and experiences I have desired. I am still working hard towards many more goals. Pushing these dreams aside to raise a child is something I do not want to do.

Reason #51
I Don't Like The Human Species

At the end of the day, I just simply don't like humans. I believe we are a horrible species that doesn't deserve to exist and I won't add to the population.

Responses I'm Tired of Hearing

Response #1
"You'll Change Your Mind"

This is one response that immediately gets my blood boiling. I have heard this response countless times, and I am tired of it. Yes, it is possible for people to change their minds about this decision and plenty of people do. But that doesn't mean everyone will change their minds. Thinking you know someone better than they know themselves and telling them they will change their minds is, in my opinion, incredibly disrespectful and arrogant.

Response #2
"You'll Regret It When You Are Older"

It is certainly possible to regret a decision like this and some people do end up regretting the choice not to have children. But not everyone who chooses a childfree life regrets it. We are all different and all have our own reasons for making this choice. There is no possible way to predict who will and who won't regret it in fifty years.

Most childfree individuals are aware of this possibility. I, and many others, took this into consideration while making our decisions. I am well-aware that I might turn eighty and suddenly come to regret not having any babies. I know this is a possibility, and I am fine with that. I accept that there is a chance I might regret my choice and that I might regret it at an age where I can no longer change my mind.

What I am not okay with is the possibility of regretting the choice to have children. Having a child is a permanent decision that involves an innocent human being. Every child deserves to grow up feeling wanted, and I am not okay with the possibility that I could not provide that for my child. I was lucky enough to be raised by a mother who spoke quite often of how much she desired my sibling and me. How my mother had my name picked out years before becoming pregnant with me. How if she could go back in time and change things, she wouldn't. How raising us was the most joyous thing she had done with her life. I have no idea what it would feel like to be raised by parents who regretted having me. I imagine it would feel horrible. Many people experience this and I refuse to risk the possibility of subjecting a child to my regret. Regretting not having kids involves me, and only me. Regretting having kids involves innocent children.

Response #3
"Who Will Take Care Of You When You Are Old?"

I don't know who will take care of me in my old age. But if I had to guess, I think it will be the staff at a classy nursing home. A nice one that I can afford with the money I didn't spend on babies. One with friendly and caring workers that will treat me well. Or I might be able to afford in-home care until my passing. That would be even better.

Children are individuals, not retirement plans, and they have no obligation to plan for their parent's future. We are all responsible for our own lives and retirements. We should teach children to plan for their own retirement, starting early in life. In this economy, even if I wanted to be my parent's retirement plan, I cannot afford to. I have had to work hard to pay off cars and student loans, working full time to keep myself out of debt. I have my own future to plan for, I cannot plan for anybody else's.

Even if I was willing to bring a sentient life form into existence for the sole purpose of being my caretaker, there is no guarantee they will take care of me. Untimely deaths happen every day, my children could die before me and I will still be responsible for my own retirement care. There is also the possibility that my children will not like me enough to become my caretaker. Many children choose to cut off contact with their parents for a variety of reasons. If my children choose to cut me off, I will still be responsible for my retirement. Even families who get along great sometimes end up living far apart from each other. If I live a thousand miles away from my children, once again, I am still responsible for my own retirement. Children are not a reliable form of retirement plan, nor do they have any obligation to care for elderly parents.

Response #4
"You Aren't A Real Adult Until You Have Kids"

Adult: *noun*
A person who is fully grown or developed.

Legally we become adults at the age of eighteen and physically our brains do not fully develop until age twenty-five. So, anyone aged twenty-five and older is a "real" adult according to the definition of the word. No kids required.

Response #5
"What If Your Spouse Wants Kids?"

I would never marry someone who wanted kids.

Response #6
"Your Parents Deserve/Want Grandchildren"

I do not owe my parents anything. It is not my responsibility to provide grandchildren for anyone, and I refuse to ruin my life so they can have a little entertainment.

Response #7
"Life Has No Meaning If You Don't Have Kids"

It is my opinion that the only meaning life has is the meaning we choose to give it. Everyone can feel differently about what the meaning of their life is, but I give my life meaning by choosing things that bring me joy, doing things that make others happy, and by rescuing as many animals as I can. Maybe you feel that your life has no meaning without kids, and I'm sorry if you feel that way, but that does not give you, or anyone, the right to tell others that their lives have no meaning.

On a similar note, my life is not worth any less if I choose not to have kids. I have been told that there is no point in my being alive because of my decision, that I am a waste of a human being. The idea that someone is only valuable because of their reproductive capabilities, is incredibly dehumanizing.

I am worth more than my organs. I am more important than my ability to breed.

Response #8
"It's Selfish To Not Have Kids"

I don't believe making decisions about my own body and life, that have no effect on anyone else, is selfish.

Response #9
"What A Waste, There Are So Many Infertile Women"

First, I've never tried to get pregnant, so I actually don't know if I am fertile or infertile. Second, birthing a child of my own does not help infertile women in any way. Third, by this logic, should I consume peanuts every day of my life so as not to waste my peanut enjoying abilities because there are so many people with peanut allergies who are incapable of enjoying peanuts?

Response #10
"You'll Be Lonely When You Get Old"

As an introvert who highly cherishes time spent by myself, I highly doubt that. In any case, having kids is no guarantee that someone won't be lonely as they age. Nursing homes are full of parents who experience loneliness when their children are too busy to visit.

Response #11
"Don't You Want To Pass On Your Genetics/Family Name?"

Family names are a human construct and don't have any meaning, so I see no point in passing them along. Humans are the only creatures on this planet that seem to care about surnames. Also, as a woman, the patriarchy has decided that I am not worthy of passing on names.

Genetics are also something I have no interest in passing on and believe that this reason is not a valid excuse to have a child. Even if I cared about my genetic traits being passed on to the next generation, I don't have particularly special DNA. I am incapable of seeing without using bent pieces of glass to look through, have anxiety if forced to speak over a telephone, struggle to breathe if I run too long, have a mild sugar addiction, and my genetic mutation of an eye color makes it difficult to see in bright lights. My genetics are not worth passing on.

Response #12
"But Having Kids Is The Best Part Of Life!"

I will never understand why parents think that wiping someone else's butt and driving a minivan is the best part of life. Although, if someone is truly happy spending their time raising children, then I think that's what they should do. But the "best part of life" is different for everyone, and we all enjoy different things. The "best part of life" for me is traveling and exploring the natural wonders of the world. That's what I want to spend my time doing.

Response #13
"You'll Meet A Man And Just Want To Have His Babies"

My response to this statement as a 15-year-old: I doubt it.

My response to this statement as a 30-year-old: Well. I've met a man, married him, bought a house, and settled down. I have yet to have an overwhelming desire to have his babies.

Response #14
"Don't You Want To Leave A Legacy/ Be Remembered?"

The desire to be remembered, and the use of children to accomplish said desire, is a concept that I truly do not understand. Why do we, as humans, strive so hard to accomplish things for the sole purpose of being remembered? Why is it so important to leave a legacy? Other animals strive to pass on their genetic material but they do not write their names anywhere in an effort to be remembered. Why are humans the exception?

An individual has to do something incredibly good or incredibly bad to make it into a history book. And even then, how long before the history books forget you? If you don't make it into a history book and are remembered only by your children, how many generations before they forget your name? Three? Four? Five if you are lucky? Someday your name will only be discussed when a distant grandchild is required to do a genealogy report in middle school (And they will probably laugh at how old-fashioned sounding your name was).

The world will forget you, whether it takes one hundred years or one thousand years. This is not a sad thing or a bad thing, it is just a part of life. We are living on a floating rock in space. Someday the sun will explode and there will be no trace of this planet left behind. Nothing really matters and we are all going to die. I don't think it's worth trying so hard to be remembered by people who will forget you. Considering the fact that it probably won't work, having a child for the sake of being remembered seems like a poor reason to have a kid.

Let's do a quick experiment.
Absolutely no cheating! (That means you can't ask your parents or look up the answers online.)

What are your parents' names?
What are your grandparents' names?
What are your great-grandparents' names?
What are your great-great-grandparents' names?
What are your great-great-great-grandparents' names?
What are your great-great-great-great-grandparents' names?

How many generations before names are forgotten?

Response #15
"You'll Get Bigger Tax Returns"

The overall cost of raising a child is much larger than any tax return you may get. So not only is this a mathematically bad reason to reproduce, but I believe it is also an ethically bad reason. If someone only gives birth to or fosters children for the money, I have to question the quality of care the child will be receiving. When people only care about profits, too many corners start getting cut. And it's the children who are the ones to suffer the consequences of others' greed.

Response #16
"Don't You Want To See What They Would Look Like?"

I don't think "to see what they would look like" is a valid reason to have children. I will not sign up for eighteen or more years of responsibility just to see what my kids would look like. Besides, my husband is handsome and I am beautiful, so there is no doubt our children would be just as attractive. And if I really am that curious about what my kids would look like, there are websites and apps that can merge mine and my partner's photos together for free.

Response #17
"You Aren't A 'Real' Family Until You Have Kids"

While the traditional meaning of family is a mother, a father, and one or more children, modern times seem to be changing that definition. A mother and father with children has always been, and always will be, considered a family. But recent generations seem to be redefining the term to include other types of families as well. There are a million different ways to define "family" and they do not always require children.

Friends that accept you more than your blood relatives are family. Two mothers and their children are a family. Two fathers and their children are a family. A single person and their pet are a family. Individuals that co-parent platonically are a family. A couple with pets instead of children is a family. Single parents and their children are a family. A polycule with or without children is a family. A couple with no kids and no pets are a family. My husband, myself, and our pets are a tiny, happy family. We do not need your approval to experience true love or a real family.

Response #18
"Just Have One And See If You Like It"

The people who say this to me honestly scare me. Do people seriously have such little regard for the consequences of their actions? What if I have a baby, don't like it, and now some poor innocent child has to be raised by a parent who doesn't want them? Every child deserves to be wanted and the children are the ones who suffer in these situations. Having children is a permanent decision, and I can't just put it back into my uterus if I decide that having kids isn't for me.

Response #19
"What If Your Parents Had Felt The Same Way?"

If my parents had felt the same way I do, and had chosen a childfree life, then I would not exist. I would be unaware of this thing we call life and would never have been annoyed enough to write this book. And since I wouldn't exist, I would not even be aware of not existing, so I wouldn't care that I didn't exist.

Response #20
"You'll Have A Hard Time Finding A Spouse"

I was incredibly vocal about my decision to be childfree with every person I ever dated and I still ended up married by twenty-three. Personally, I found that being childfree made dating easier. I had the "do you want kids" discussion within the first two weeks of all my relationships. Meaning that most of them didn't last very long, but that's okay. I didn't want to waste either of our time with dating if it was going to end because of differences, like wanting or not wanting kids. Not wanting kids is a major deal-breaker for many people and I always wanted to be open about my desires before we developed serious feelings toward each other. It's easier to end a two-week relationship than a two-year relationship.

Response #21
"If Everyone Chose Not To Have Children, The Human Race Would Die Out!"

I want to be perfectly clear on this one. If I were the last human female capable of reproduction, and the fate of the entire human race rested with my uterus, I still wouldn't have kids. I would gladly end the human race with a smile on my face. Humans don't deserve to exist. It is not my responsibility to keep the human race going, and honestly, the Earth would be better off without us.

Response #22
"But Childbirth Is Such A Miracle!"

<u>Miracle</u>: *noun*
A surprising and welcome event that is not explicable by natural or scientific laws and therefore considered to be the work of a divine agency.

Since childbirth is well understood and can be explained by science, it is by definition, not a miracle. Every living thing on this planet is capable of reproduction, the fact that humans can do it too is not special. Even if childbirth was, by definition a miracle, I still fail to see why that is a valid reason to participate in the activity.

Response #23
*"Accidents Happen *wink* *wink*"*

It is not by accident that I have made it to thirty years old without any pregnancies. Excluding cases of rape and sexual assault, anyone who is old enough to be participating in sexual intercourse should be aware that pregnancy is a possible outcome. Anyone who does not wish for a pregnancy to occur should be using proper contraceptives. I can honestly say that I have never in my entire life had unprotected sex for fear of becoming pregnant. But yes, every form of birth control has the possibility of failing, resulting in accidental pregnancies. This is why reproductive rights are so important, anyone who wants or needs an abortion should have access to them.

Response #24
"Pregnancy/Childbirth Really Isn't That Bad, You'll Forget About The Pain"

I wholeheartedly disagree. Please see Reason #4 for further information.

Response #25
"But You Would Be Such A Great Mom"

Thanks, but just because I might be good at something, doesn't mean I'm required to do it. I also would have been a great artist, but I choose to pursue other career interests. I don't regret my choice to follow a different career path, just like I don't regret my choice not to be a mom, even though I might have been a good one.

Response #26
"I Hope You Get Pregnant On Accident"

I think that wishing something upon someone while knowing that individual doesn't want it, is terribly cruel. If I were to somehow experience an accidental pregnancy, it would result in an immediate abortion. Which is something that can cause both physical and emotional traumas. I wouldn't wish an unwanted pregnancy or an abortion upon my worst enemy.

Response #27
"You Won't Know What True Love Is Until You Have Children"

True love exists in many forms. I love my husband, my parents, my sibling, my pets, and my friends. Each love is different, but each love is still "true." I don't think I need to shove a baby out of my vagina to understand what love is. Motherly love is not the only form of love, and you don't need to have a child to understand it.

Response #28
"You Must Hate Kids"

Just because someone chooses not to reproduce or raise their own child, does not mean that they hate kids. Many childfree people enjoy being around children. Some even choose careers centered around childcare. Choosing a childfree life has nothing to do with whether-or-not someone likes or dislikes kids. But me personally? Yeah, I hate kids.

Response #29
"Adopted Kids Are Not Your Real Kids"

For a few years in my teens, I was open to the idea of adopting children. I was still unsure of whether-or-not I might change my mind. But I knew for certain that if I had kids, I would not be having them myself. Never in my life have I ever had the desire to experience pregnancy or childbirth. Someday, if I was ever ready, I would adopt children instead of birthing them.

Every single time I have told someone that I

did not want biological children, they would respond with *"If you adopt, they won't be your real kids though"* or *"I would have difficulty loving a child that wasn't mine."* This is a view that I have never and will never understand. Having children means loving them unconditionally. And if you need your own blood running through their veins to love them, that is conditional love. If you have conditions for loving your child, I don't see you as someone fit to be a parent.

Eventually, I changed my mind about wanting to adopt children; I enjoy my childfree life too much to change it. Looking back, the only reason I wanted to adopt kids was because I wanted to help them, not because I wanted the experience of raising or parenting a child. I just wanted to help some kids get out of a difficult situation. I had dreams of adopting siblings to prevent them from being separated. But I never actually wanted to be a mother. I just desperately wanted to provide a home for someone who needed one. But there are other ways to help these kids rather than adoption, such as becoming an advocate, volunteering, or monetary donations.

Special thanks to all the adoptive and foster parents out there. The world needs more people with such big hearts. And as always, no matter how your child comes into your life, they will always be your real children.

Response #30
"Having Kids Is Good For The Economy"

Can you imagine ever telling a child that the only reason they exist is to stimulate the economy?

Also, I don't care about the economy.

Response #31
"Have A Kid And You'll Have A Friend For Life"

I am already capable of making friends on my own. Are you so bad at building friendships that you have to literally make a friend? One who is entirely dependent on you and legally cannot run away for the first eighteen years? One who might have a touch of Stockholm Syndrome? Perhaps you should work on your people skills before using this as an excuse to have a kid. Plus, there is no guarantee that my child will want to be my friend. My kid might hate me for any number of reasons. I don't think birthing a child for the sake of friendship is a very sound idea.

Response #32
"You'll Never Truly Be Financially Ready, So Just Go For It"

This is a response I hear fairly often when I say that I cannot afford kids. And it baffles me that so many people are this irresponsible when it comes to deciding whether-or-not to have children. I understand kids are extremely expensive, but what if I had this attitude towards other things? I would love to own expensive cars and houses. Should I purchase these things even if I am not financially prepared? No lender would ever approve me for loans I couldn't handle.

"It's never the right time, so you just gotta go for it. Things have a way of working themselves out. All kids really need is love, you can figure out the

money part later." This is a statement from a family member when they were trying to convince me to have children. My own family thinks that it is acceptable to have kids even if you are fully aware that you are not financially ready for them. And I think that choosing to reproduce when you know you are not properly prepared to care for them, is an incredibly selfish and irresponsible thing to do.

Response #33
"Having Kids Will Make You Happier"

While this statement might be true for some people, for many parents, it is quite the opposite. Of course, every parent feels differently about their experiences with parenthood, and there are many varying factors such as age, location, and wealth. But quite a few of them end up being less happy than they were before they had children. I know for myself, having kids would not make me happier, it would make me a great deal less happy.

Response #34
"But We Need More White Babies"

That's just racist.

Response #35
"You're Running Out Of Time..."

As I've entered my thirties, this is a new response that I am starting to encounter. As if thirty is too late to start a family. Plenty of people choose to wait until later in life before having or adopting kids, and there is nothing wrong with that. There is no magical "right" age to begin parenthood. And since I have already decided that I am never going to have kids, there is no time crunch. There is no clock to race against. I couldn't care less if my "biological clock" is ticking because I never had plans to use my uterus anyway. There is no way for me to "run out of time" to have children if I never planned on having them in the first place.

Response #36
"What Will You Do With Your Life If You Don't Have Kids?"

I will have fun! I will spend my money on exciting vacations and stupid trinkets. I'll get drunk whenever I want. I'll stay up until three in the morning and sleep in until noon. I'll have sex whenever and wherever I want. I'll watch R-rated movies and visit sex shops. I'll adopt as many pets as I can afford. I'll read good books and eat delicious food. I'll spend time with friends and family. I'll write books and cry when they don't sell. I'll marvel at the beauty of nature. I'll hike in the rain and watch storms from my porch. I'll plant gardens and watch them grow. I'll listen to loud music and drive too fast. I'll buy the house of my dreams. I'll yell at strangers for littering and volunteer at beach cleanups. I'll spend time with my spouse. I'll dance naked in my living room and watch movies with no pants on. I will do anything my heart desires! I'll live my life to the fullest I can while dreaming about even bigger and better things in my future.

Response #37
"Do You Regret It?"

The first time someone asked me this question, I was twenty-nine years old, and it caught me completely by surprise. I didn't think I was old enough to regret it yet, didn't think late twenties were too late to change my mind if I wanted to. As of right now, no, I do not regret my decision and I honestly love my childfree life. But I am only thirty years old, and don't think I can accurately answer this question yet. I need to become a senior before I can truly know the answer. Ask me again in fifty years.

Things About Parenthood That Annoy Me

Annoying Thing #1
Gender Reveal Parties

Since sex and gender are two different things, let's call these parties what they actually are, sex reveal parties. The term "sex" refers to physical body parts such as penises and vaginas. And the term "gender" refers to the socially constructed roles, expressions, and behaviors of individuals. Not only are sex reveal parties just the beginning of a lifetime full of conscious or unconsciously forced gender roles, they can also be quite dangerous or destructive activities.

These generally quiet and fun events hosted in homes or backyards have been known to get disastrously out of control and result in extensive damages or even death. Sex reveal parties have caused catastrophes such as wildfires, plane crashes, earthquake-like property damage, and deaths. So, if we could please let these parties that reinforce potentially harmful gender roles and cause physical damages to go out of style and never come back, that would be great.

Annoying Thing #2
Baby Showers

I've been to a handful of baby showers, and they were not the best experiences for me. I find them to be incredibly boring and repetitive, with the same unoriginal games at each party. From spending hours pretending to be excited about another little crotch goblin to fielding questions about when I will be having my own baby, I rarely have a good time. Usually only attending out of a feeling of obligation. And, even though it's not my kid, I am expected to spend money on a gift for it. Risking looking like a cheapskate if I choose the least expensive item on the baby registry. I'll be happy if I never attend another baby shower for the rest of my life.

Annoying Thing #3
The Idea That I Cannot Comprehend Certain Things Because I Am Not A Parent

"You don't have kids so you don't know what it's like to love like a mother." I have been told that I am incapable of understanding certain things because I don't have children. I completely disagree. Obviously, I do not and will never know what it is like to give birth to a baby and raise it for eighteen years. But I believe I do not need to squeeze a tiny human out of my vagina to understand motherly love. I have experienced maternal love multiple times in my life, towards both humans and animals. I may not have any human children of my own, but I have loved countless animals. And know what it is like to make sure their needs are met before my own. Putting their health and safety before my own, isn't that what motherly love is?

My own pets I have watched grow from newborns, through adulthood, to becoming seniors and passing away. Watching them grow and play, teaching them about the world. Isn't that part of being a mother? I have also fostered many newborn animals. It is such a joy to experience this kind of thing, watching these tiny, helpless babies grow into adults each with their own personality. I have gotten up in the middle of the night to do feedings. I have stimulated orphan bellies and cleaned their dirty bottoms when they had no mother of their own to do it for them. I have provided them love and care and then had to say goodbye and hope they do well on their own when they go out into the world. How is this not motherly love? The immediate and unconditional love that I feel, how is it not maternal love?

And even if this type of love "isn't the same" because it's animals, not humans, I know what it is like to love the human children in my life. I have loved, lived with, and bonded with many kids throughout my life. I have been a friend, and I have been a mother figure. I know what it's like to play and be happy with them. I know what it's like to sit and brush the tangles out of their hair. I know the joy of showing them the wonders of the world. To hold their tiny hands. To comfort them when they are hurt or scared. To accompany them to the bathroom. I know what it is like to chase them around the house in an attempt to tire them out enough to tuck them into bed. I know the joy of seeing them run into my arms when they are excited to see me. How are these not motherly experiences? I may not be their mother, but I want nothing but the best for these children. Just because I have not mothered my own human child does not mean I haven't mothered.

"You'll never understand true tiredness until you have kids." Exhaustion is another thing that parents seem to think only applies to them. The idea that parents believe they are the only ones who can experience being truly tired or overwhelmed is baffling. I'm sure that everyone on the planet has felt true exhaustion at some point or another in their lives. It's true the constant care that children require can be quite exhausting, but if parents did proper research before deciding to have kids, they would know to expect this. Just because I don't have children

doesn't mean I don't know what being tired is.

"You think you're busy? Try being a parent!" While it's true that juggling all the responsibilities associated with being a parent can leave you with an incredibly busy schedule, non-parents can also have hectic schedules. Some people have busy careers that demand large amounts of time. Some people have to take care of sick or old family members. Some people have to juggle multiple jobs to make ends meet, while also dealing with hectic personal lives. Not having kids isn't a guarantee of constant free time.

Whether it's maternal love, exhaustion, being busy, or something else, just because someone is not a parent doesn't mean that they are incapable of understanding or experiencing them.

Annoying Thing #4
The Phrase "We Are Trying For A Baby"

Why is it socially acceptable for someone to say "we are trying for a baby" in public, but I can't say "my husband is raw-dogging me every night for recreational purposes?" I don't need or want to know that you are having unprotected sex for the sake of reproduction. Please keep it to yourselves.

Annoying Thing #5
Parents Who Don't Teach Their Children Animal Safety

Most humans interact with animals on a daily basis. Whether pets or wildlife, we share this planet with animals and we have to learn how to interact with them respectfully and safely. It is a parent's responsibility to teach their children how to behave around animals, for everyone's safety.

I have taught my pets to be respectful of humans, but they are still animals capable of biting and clawing. Animals have personalities and boundaries just like people and deserve to be treated with respect. And if we choose to share our lives with them, it is our responsibility to learn how to communicate with them properly. Animals have warning behaviors for a reason. I would never blame my pets for any aggression towards myself if I ignored their physical or vocal warnings. I expect strangers and their children to give my pets this same respect. Children should also be taught to ask permission before approaching or touching someone else's animals.

These boundaries apply to wildlife as well as domesticated animals. Wild animals are not pets, and they will not hesitate to defend themselves from perceived dangers. Too many kids are hurt or killed each year because they are not taught proper animal safety. Teach your children how to behave correctly around animals, both wild and domestic.

Annoying Thing #6

Making Every Possible Effort To Change My Mind

When the words "I don't want kids" come out of my mouth, some people seem to take it as a personal challenge to change my mind. I end up having excruciatingly long conversations with friends, family, and even strangers about my lifestyle choice. I don't understand why it is so important to people that I have children. Why it is so essential to convince one girl from rural Ohio to have a baby? When I tell people I don't want pet birds, nobody tries to persuade me to change my mind about that. I support childfree people and would love to see more individuals choosing not to have biological kids, but everyone has the right to choose for themselves, and I would never go out of my way to try to persuade someone not to have kids. So please, stop trying to convince childfree people to change their minds.

Annoying Thing #7
Showing To Many Photos/Videos

I understand parents think their child is the cutest and most special child on the planet. I get it; I think the same thing about my pets. But please, for the love of God, limit the photo/video sharing to one. I cannot handle looking at a hundred photos of the same kid doing something boring. And if you show me a video that is longer than thirty seconds long, please know that I hate you. I am smiling and nodding and saying things like "how cute" out of politeness. I'm trying not to hurt your feelings but I don't think your kid is cute and I don't care that they learned to crawl or walk or poop or talk. Please learn when to recognize when other people just aren't interested.

Annoying Thing #8
Parents That Keep Having Kids Until They Get The Sex They Want

If I think that choosing to have biological children is selfish, the only thing more egocentric is continually reproducing until you have a child with the specific set of genitalia desired.

Annoying Thing #9
Unnecessarily Large Number Of Children

There is no magic "right" number of kids that make a perfect-sized family. But when parents choose to continue having an unnecessary amount of babies, eventually there will be too many for the parents to give each child the proper amount of care. It can become difficult or impossible for the traditional two parents to provide enough quality time and emotional support when there are too many children in the family. Often, the older children are forced to step into parental roles and begin caring for their younger siblings. These older siblings should not spend their childhoods filling the roles their parents are unable to fill. No child should have to become caregivers for their siblings because their parents had too many babies. It is incredibly selfish on the parents' part.

Annoying Thing #10
Dumping Pets When Baby Comes Along

Understandably, unexpected situations can always arise. Responsibly re-homing a pet into an appropriate and safe environment is sometimes necessary if current living conditions could cause harm to either animals or humans. But finding a new home for a pet with competent friends or family differs vastly from dumping them at the nearest animal shelter or releasing them into the wild. Pets are not disposable accessories that can be thrown out or traded in when it's convenient. Getting rid of a pet just because you have a baby on the way or said baby is taking up too much of your time, is selfish and unacceptable behavior. Animals are a time and financial commitment, and whether-or-not you plan on having future children is something that should be taken into consideration before adopting.

Annoying Thing #11
Strangers That Wish Me A "Happy Mother's Day"

Every year, without fail, a stranger wishes me a *"Happy Mother's Day!"* And every year I make a stranger feel awkward by replying with *"I'm not a mom."* They usually respond with something along the lines of *"Oh sorry, I didn't know"* and scurry off a little embarrassed. I know most people mean well, but is it so hard to just ask someone if they are a mother before saying something like that? For someone like me, this experience is a slight annoyance. For someone who is struggling with infertility or child loss, it could break their heart. Think before you speak.

Annoying Thing #12
Using Friends As Baby Sitters

When I was in high school, one of my classmates had a baby. She was one of my neighbors and we would hang out after school fairly often. She was my friend, and I still wanted to spend time with her even though she had a newborn. But after the baby arrived, we didn't do fun things anymore. I would end up watching an infant I had no qualifications to supervise while she took showers or did household chores. I was being used as a free babysitter.

I still wanted to be friends, but not if I was going to be exploited at every turn. Eventually, I stopped visiting, and we drifted apart. I know parents warn each other about losing friends when you have children but maybe it's because the friends don't like the way new parents treat them. Obviously, not all parents do this, but it still was an unpleasant experience to go through. If you want me to babysit your kid, please, just ask. I'm going to say "no" but still, it's polite.

Annoying Thing #13
The Idea That Having Kids Would Change My Opinions On Controversial Topics

"You would feel differently if you had kids."
"Would you teach that to your children if you had them?"
"You'll get more conservative when you have children."

The idea that I would change my beliefs if I had children bewilders me. When telling people I believe in LGBT+ rights, feminism, or racial equality, I am often met with a response such as *"But would you teach that to your children if you had them?"* Of course I would. If I believe in equality for all regardless of race, gender, or sexual orientation, I would certainly teach those beliefs to my hypothetical children. Why do parents think I would change my views if I reproduced?

These statements are similar to the statement *"You'll get more conservative as you get older."* And oh man, do I get less and less conservative with each passing day.

Honorable Mentions

Honorable Mention #1
Doubt

  I am extremely confident in my decision to be childfree. I have done all the research and know all the reasons why I don't want children. I have explained them countless times over the last fifteen years and I'm sure I will continue to have to explain myself for years to come. But facing so much opposition about this decision means that no matter how sure I am about myself, I still occasionally experience doubt.

  If so many people feel I am wrong, maybe I am wrong. What if I made the wrong choice? Is it too late to change my mind? Seeing mothers on social media looking so happy with their children, should I have chosen that? All the beautiful moments I experience with the children in my life, should I be having those moments with my own child? On the few occasions where a child has accidentally called me "Mommy," I wondered what it would be like for my own child to call me that? Are these my true feelings or are they my natural urges to reproduce? Is this real or just instincts? Is this real or is it just a fear of missing out? Or am I just bored with my life right now and want something to do?

  This is a serious lifestyle choice, and making the wrong decision can lead to a lot of grief. I may look confident in front of others about my decision, but I have shed countless tears of indecision, fear, heartache, and sadness behind closed doors. I have felt conflicted and alone, like nobody understood what I was feeling. But meeting other childfree people has let me know that I am far from alone in this world. There are always others who have gone through similar things. Not every childfree person experiences doubt, but some do, and that's normal. There is nothing wrong with having doubts. Ultimately, this is a decision that only you can make for yourself. Nobody else can make it for you. I made this decision for myself. This is my life and my choice. I choose to do what makes me happy.

Honorable Mention #2
Lack Of Childfree Books In Physical Bookstores

When I read books, I exclusively read physical copies, and I prefer to hold them in my hand before deciding to purchase. So when I decided to look for books about the childfree lifestyle, I began at bookstores and libraries. But living in a relatively small town means that we don't have any major bookstores. I have to drive two towns over to get to the nearest large, nationwide bookstore. And when I asked if they had any books about being childfree, I was told they had none. They did have a couple hundred books on parenting, though. Even visiting local libraries left me with only one physical book available to check out. The next place to search was online, and that is where I had some luck.

Finding books that are exclusively about the deliberate choice not to have children, and not about struggling with or accepting childlessness, can be difficult even online. There are hardly any of these books available compared to the number of parenting books that are easily accessible. Childfree books do have a much smaller target audience, but with each generation having more and more people choosing not to raise kids, you'd think there would be more books about it by now. I appreciate and thank every author who wrote about their experiences with this choice before me. But seeing a lack of childfree books, especially in physical stores, inspired me to write one. Hopefully, someone relates to and enjoys this book.

Honorable Mention #3
Guilt Over Not Adopting

Some people say that not having children is a selfish thing to do. That statement is false and I will never understand why people think that way. I have never and will never feel bad or guilty about my decision to live a childfree life. But one thing I do feel guilty about is my decision not to adopt. I am a thirty-year-old woman in a healthy marriage. I own a three-bedroom house with a small yard. We are not rich but my spouse and I both have steady incomes. I technically have space for two children. I could choose to adopt two kids who need a home. I could give them all the unconditional love and support they could ever need. I could pull two kids out of the often abusive foster care system. I could make two children happy. And yet, I choose not to.

This is the decision I feel immense guilt over. I choose vacations and extra spending money over helping two children. For that, I am sorry. For every child that has ever gone through or will go through the foster care system, I am sorry I didn't help you. If I could provide loving families for all of you, I would. The only thing that makes me feel better about this guilt is knowing that I would not be happy as a parent, which would make me a bad parent. And the children in foster care deserve good parents. Every child deserves good parents.

If anyone reading this is currently in the

system, please know that it is not your fault that you ended up there. And it is not your fault that the system fails so often. You deserve so much more. Remember, you are worthy of love and family. Your family will find you someday, even if you have to wait until after you become an adult. They are out there. Please be patient.

Honorable Mention #4
Pregnancy Test Ads

The overwhelming majority of pregnancy test advertisements usually depict women who are extremely happy to see their positive results. It would be nice to see more advertisers showing ads about people who are happy to see a negative test result. Even people who do eventually want children have probably taken tests when they were not ready for kids and hoped for negative results. The handful of times I have had to take pregnancy tests, I was full of panic and terror. Those few minutes of waiting on test results were far from happy moments. Childfree people are still a minority but we are a growing minority and I would love to see some more representation for us.

Honorable Mention #5
Vasectomies

I'd like to take a moment to praise all the men who have had vasectomies for any reason. Thank you for taking responsibility for your own bodies and actions. Most women who use birth control have to deal with very difficult physical and emotional side effects. And sterilizations for women are often inaccessible for the people who want them. Vasectomies are much more accessible, affordable, and easier to perform than sterilizations for people with uteruses. In most cases, they heal quickly with little to no complications. They can even be fairly easily reversed if the man decides he wants to have children. And despite what some may believe, vasectomies, or any other form of sterilization does not make anyone "less of a man."

I am immensely grateful to my husband who received a vasectomy when I had my long-term birth control removed. He is the reason I no longer have to spend money on contraception, deal with any kind of side effects, or have to use condoms anymore. Making sex more enjoyable and less stressful for me. Having a sterilized partner has eased my anxiety about any unwanted pregnancies and has allowed my body to have healthier, more natural menstrual cycles. Thank you, love!

Honorable Mention #6
Childless Vs Childfree

<u>Childless</u>: *adjective*
Not having children

<u>Childfree</u>: *adjective*
Not having any children, especially by choice

These two words are similar and are often used interchangeably, which can irritate both childless and childfree individuals. Technically, both terms could apply to someone like me, but over the years they have begun to describe two different types of people. "Childless" refers to individuals who want children, but for some reason do not have them. "Childfree" refers to individuals who do not want children and do not have them.

Why does it matter? Because the words we use to describe ourselves are important. "Childless" is often seen as a negative or unwanted label. Childless people did not choose a life without children and are generally saddened by it. "Childfree" is used as a positive or desired label. Childfree individuals choose this life of freedom from children and are joyful about it. We childfree folk see our decision as something to be happy about. We do not think of our lives as "less" because of the absence of children. We choose this life. We want this life. We are childfree, not childless.

Of course, not every label fits everyone the same and people should use the label they are most comfortable with.

Honorable Mention #7
Anyone Can Have Kids

It blows my mind that nearly anyone can just make a baby whenever they want. I can't drive a motorized vehicle or own a dog without a license but I can make a baby without consulting anyone? At this point, there should be some kind of basic child care test to prove that you are capable of keeping a child alive and healthy. It can even happen by accident, you can accidentally create a sentient life form. I wish I could accidentally make pizzas.

Honorable Mention #8
Open Availability

An incredibly frustrating thing I have encountered with employers is the idea that I have open availability because I don't have children. Parents and non-parents are often treated very differently in the workplace. Companies have reputations for not treating parents very well either, but this is my experience as a non-parent.

Bosses assume I am available to cover any shift when someone else calls off to take their sick kid to the doctor. Just because I don't have children doesn't mean I want or am able to cover any shift with no notice. I have a life outside of work with a variety of other commitments. Why is it acceptable for some workers to come in late every day because they have to drop a kid off at school, but the second I need extra time off to take my pet to the veterinarian, I become a bad employee?

Honorable Mention #9
Media With A Baby As The Happy Ending

As someone who has spent an excessive amount of time watching television and reading books, I'm tired of seeing the same cliché happy ending of falling in love and having a baby. Even when I choose a book or movie specifically because it has no romance, the last two pages or five minutes will be about the main character's happy ending of marriage and a baby on the way. I understand that for most people, this is a happy ending. But when I see these endings, I just roll my eyes. Not everyone needs a baby or a marriage to be happy.

My other problem with mainstream media is the lack of true representation. Good childfree representation in media does exist, and for that, I am grateful. But very often, these characters end up changing their minds about wanting children. They accidentally get pregnant or become saddened by the news of being infertile. Somehow, most childfree characters end up with children whether-or-not they want it. Having all these characters change their minds or suddenly be okay with accidental pregnancies reinforces the stereotype that all childfree people will change their minds. Which is one of the many reasons people like me are met with disbelief and bombarded with so many questions about our lifestyle choice. I beg the authors and directors of the world, if you choose to have childfree representation in your work, please make sure it is an accurate representation.

Honorable Mention #10
My One Regret

My only regret in life is not getting sterilized the day I turned eighteen. I had great health insurance at the time and I would have healed wonderfully. Then I wouldn't have had to spend so much of my life being terrified of an unwanted pregnancy. I should have gotten my entire uterus removed since there's no point in me having one. For an organ I will never use, it has extremely expensive maintenance, is incredibly painful, and annoyingly inconvenient. Dealing with monthly menstruation knowing I'm not even going to get any use out of my reproductive organs infuriates me to no end. So if anyone reading this has access to a time machine, please give me a call.

Honorable Mention #11
A Plea To Others To Stop Asking Such Personal Questions

There is nothing wrong with having personal discussions between people who are willing to be open with each other. But when it comes to finding out that someone does not want to have children, suddenly every friend, family member, coworker, and stranger feels they have the right to demand answers to incredibly personal questions. Some people don't mind answering these questions, but many people simply don't want to discuss the topic.

I am exhausted from fifteen years of having to repeat the same answers to the same questions or responses. Most days these questions will immediately anger me, and at this point, I am no longer capable of having these conversations calmly. I will be rude and mean to people who demand I explain my reasons for not reproducing, which of course makes me the "aggressively childfree" person. Some days, I can laugh and joke about my lifestyle with people who don't judge me for my choices. But other days, if phrased just right, these questions can feel like daggers to the heart. These questions have the ability to catch me off guard and they can tear me apart. One question can stick with me for the rest of the day and suddenly I'll be crying myself to sleep over a decision I thought I was confident in.

Being childfree would be so much easier if I didn't have to fight so hard against social norms. It would be so much easier if I didn't have to explain myself to every person in my life. So please, I am begging, for my sake and the sake of anyone else who doesn't want to have children, stop asking such personal questions. Mind your own business and leave us alone. Thank you.

Dear Reader,
Thank you for taking the time to read my book. If you enjoyed it, please leave a review and share with anyone who might also find joy in it.

About The Author

Jasmine F. Tucker lives in southwest Ohio with her husband, dog, two cats, and two gerbils. Currently working a full-time job that has nothing to do with her college degree and writing on the side. She enjoys hiking, horseback riding, and traveling. *51 Reasons I Don't Want Children, 37 Responses I'm Tired Of Hearing & 13 Things About Parenthood That Annoy Me* is her first book and she plans on writing more in the future.

Printed in Great Britain
by Amazon

10484003R00047